All About Animals
Giraffes

By Sarah Albee

Reader's Digest Young Families

Contents

Chapter 1
A Giraffe Story

Day Care

For the first four or five months of their lives, baby giraffes rest and play in small groups called crèches while their mothers search for food.

The sun is shining across the African savanna. The rainy season has finally ended. A giraffe is ready to have her baby. With a thud, a bundle falls six feet to the ground. Little Giraffe is born! The newborn calf is unhurt, and her mother nuzzles her lovingly.

About twenty minutes after she is born, Little Giraffe staggers to her feet. She wobbles a bit on her long, thin legs, but she soon grows steadier. She is already as tall as an adult man! Two little horns lie flat against her head, but they'll pop up in a week or so. For two weeks, Mother Giraffe hides her baby in the tall grass to keep her safe from lions and hyenas.

Little Giraffe spends most of the time lying down, but as her legs grow stronger, she begins to walk more and more. When she is hungry, she bleats and mews for her mother, who never wanders too far away.

Several months go by, and Little Giraffe grows quickly. She still drinks milk from her mother, but now she joins the group of other giraffes as they forage for tasty acacia leaves. She plays with her cousins and other young giraffe friends under the watchful eyes of an adult female giraffe while the rest of their mothers go off in search of food.

One day, while Little Giraffe's mother is guarding the crèche, she sounds an alarm call. With snorts and hisses, she alerts the other adults grazing nearby to come quickly. Eighteen feet above the ground, she has a great view of the plain. With her sharp eyes, Mother Giraffe has spotted a female lion creeping slowly toward the group of young giraffes. The other mothers run quickly back to the crèche. Little Giraffe races to her mother, who positions herself above her baby to protect her.

The lion stops stalking, stands up, and tosses her head. She knows very well that one swift kick from Mother Giraffe's front legs could be deadly. The lion gives up the hunt and trots away.

Giant Giraffes

The ancestors of giraffes that lived around 25 million years ago may have been even taller than giraffes are today.

A Good Defense
Some scientists believe that other kinds of animals, such as zebras and antelopes, intentionally graze near groups of giraffes. The giraffes' ability to spot danger from a distance helps protect these other animals, too.

Excuse Me!

Giraffes burp a lot. It's the way they release the gaseous wastes from all the leaves they eat!

Five years go by, and Little Giraffe is now fully grown. She ambles the plains with a group of other giraffes, munching leaves high above the ground and calling to the other giraffes from great distances to let them know where she is. She knows her friends and relatives by the markings on their coats, as each one is a bit different from another. She has also made friends with a little oxpecker bird, who loves to perch on her back and pluck annoying insects from her furry coat.

Little Giraffe will soon be ready to have a calf of her own. She will stay in the same area where her mother lives for the rest of her life.

It's a Stretch

Male and female giraffes eat leaves that grow at different heights. Males reach up to leaves growing higher than they are, with their heads and necks stretched fully upward. Females eat at the level of their body, sometimes with their head and neck slightly bent.

Chapter 2
The Body of a Giraffe

Neck and Neck

You have seven bones in your neck. So does a giraffe! The difference is that the giraffe's bones are much longer than yours!

The neck of a fully-grown giraffe is 6 to 8 feet long. That's more than the height of most adult humans!

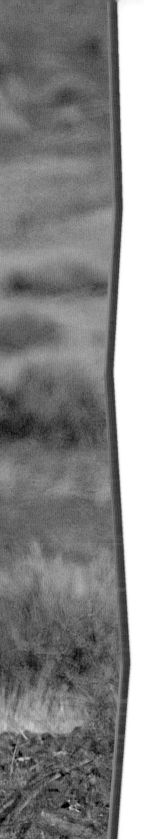

Tall and Towering

Giraffes are the tallest animals in the world. Males are 18 feet high, females 17 feet. Their height comes from their long legs and long neck.

Being the tallest animal helps giraffes survive, because they can reach food that other animals cannot. They do not have to compete with other animals for food. Their height also allows them to spot predators when they are far away, giving the giraffes time to seek safety.

Giraffes have a brown mane running the length of their necks. Their manes are short and bristly.

Giraffes have long tails with a tuft of long, stiff hair at the ends—perfect for swatting away insects.

At first glance, giraffes may look alike to us, but their coats vary quite a bit. The background color ranges from white to tan to yellowish, and giraffes' spots can be anywhere from light orange to dark brown. Also, the shape of the spots differ. One type of giraffe has large rectangular patches; others have irregular blotches. Although the pattern on a giraffe's coat remains the same throughout its life, its color darkens as the giraffe grows older.

Spot the Difference

The markings on a giraffe's coat are different on each animal. No two are exactly alike! This helps giraffes recognize one another.

Can Giraffes Jump?

Giraffes are able to jump over objects as high as 6 feet! That's about as high as a tall man!

A giraffe's front legs are longer than the back ones, giving the giraffe a slightly downward slope.

Long Legs

With its 6-foot-long legs, a giraffe can cover quite a lot of ground, even when it is just walking. You would have to run to keep up with it!

A giraffe has two strides—walking and galloping. When walking, the giraffe swings both right legs forward at the same time and then both left legs. Only one other four-legged animal walks this way—the camel! Other animals with four legs, such as dogs, walk by moving diagonally opposite legs—the front right and back left legs and then the front left and back right ones.

As it gallops, the giraffe swings its great neck backward and forward like a huge rocking horse. At a gallop, a giraffe moves 10 feet with each stride, thundering along at more than 30 miles per hour! Most of the time, though, giraffes stroll slowly, munching leaves as they go.

Giraffes have cloven feet, which means that their feet are divided in two. Their feet are covered with tough hooves. A giraffe's hoofprint is almost as long as a 12-inch ruler!

Horn of Plenty

All giraffes are born with horns on top of their heads. Some male giraffes have as many as five! As the giraffe gets older, its horns gradually grow harder and stiffer.

Sight and Smell

With their height and excellent eyesight, giraffes can see for miles across the flat African plains. Their huge brown eyes are protected by long lashes and are set on the sides of their heads so that the animal can see all around. Some animals feel safer near giraffes because they can detect predators when they are still far away. Some scientists believe that giraffes see colors quite well.

Giraffes have no tear ducts in their eyes to cleanse them. They use their long tongue to clean their eyes.

Giraffes also have a good sense of smell. A mother giraffe quickly learns to recognize her baby by the way it smells. Giraffe scent glands give off an odor that enables them to recognize one another. Their odor probably also protects them from certain bothersome insects.

Do Giraffes Make Sounds?

Many people think that giraffes are silent animals, but they are not! Although they tend to be quiet, giraffes can make a variety of sounds, such as moans, alarm calls, snorts, hisses, and flute-like notes. Baby giraffes bleat and mew. Mother giraffes, calling to their babies, may even bellow!

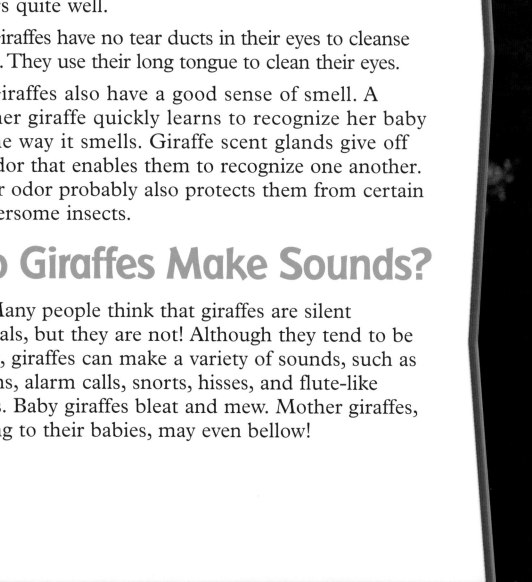

Giraffes have great hearing. Their pointy, 8-inch-long ears can swivel in several directions!

A Dozing Pose

Giraffes sometimes sleep in a sitting position, with their legs folded beneath them, but with their neck held upright.

Giraffes sometimes nap while

Catching a Few Winks

Giraffes rest after dark in an open area where they can keep a watchful eye out for danger. They lie down for a few hours to rest and ruminate (chew their cud), catching bits of sleep here and there. Giraffes usually sleep deeply for only 1 minute to 12 minutes at a time and for a total of only about 20 minutes a night. They may keep one eye open alternately to be on the alert for predators. When they do lie down and sleep, they bend their neck backward to rest on their back leg, like a handle.

Keeping Clean

Giraffes groom themselves by biting and licking. Having a 6-foot-long neck and an 18-inch-long tongue is convenient for reaching most parts of a giraffe's body!

Giraffes also have cleaning helpers—birds that live with them. The buffalo weaver and oxpecker birds perch on the giraffes and pluck out biting insects from their fur. The birds also help by calling shrilly when they spot danger.

Chapter 3
Lunch Munchers

Far Reaching

A giraffe's tongue is 18 inches long! A giraffe uses its tongue to grasp leaves that are out of its reach and to clean its eyes and ears.

Giraffes spend half of each day eating, usually in the hours before sunrise and after sunset.

Plant Eaters

Giraffes are herbivores, which means they eat only plants. The leaves of the acacia tree are their favorite. Most acacia trees have sharp thorns, sometimes 2 inches in length! But these don't bother the giraffes. With their strong, flexible lips and long, sticky tongues, the giraffes gather the leaves into their mouths and tear them off the branches by pulling their heads away.

Luckily for acacia trees, giraffes do not devour all the leaves on a tree before moving on. One reason may be the stinging ants that live in hollow areas of the acacias' branches. They protect the tree from giraffes by swarming onto their face and neck. The giraffes tolerate the stings for a short time but usually move on to the next tree.

Chewing Their Cud

Just like cows, giraffes belong to a type of animal called "ruminants." Ruminants have a stomach with four compartments that help break down the tough leaves that the animals eat.

When a giraffe is not eating, it is chewing its cud, which is a ball of partly digested leaves that travels back up the giraffe's throat into its mouth for further grinding.

A Tall Drink of Water

Drinking water is a challenging task for the world's tallest animals, because it is difficult for them to reach the level of the water.

A giraffe's front legs are so long that the giraffe must spread them far to the sides in order to lower its head to the water. This is a rather awkward position. Sometimes giraffes kneel down to drink, but this position is awkward to get in and out of, too.

Have you ever bent your head down very low (or stood on your head) and then straightened up quickly? If you have, you may have felt slightly dizzy. Imagine, then, how a giraffe feels when it lowers its head 18 feet! Fortunately, a giraffe has a special system to manage this problem. Inside the giraffe's neck are blood vessels that stretch and valves (like little trapdoors) inside the blood vessels that prevent all the blood from rushing to the animal's head as it dips way below its heart. Without these valves, the giraffe might faint every time it drinks because of the rapid changes in its blood pressure.

After a giraffe stands upright, it usually stretches its neck and back legs to get the blood flowing freely again.

Dry Spells

Like camels, giraffes can go for weeks without drinking any water. They get most of the moisture they need from the leaves they eat.

When a giraffe's legs are splayed, the giraffe is vulnerable to attack because it can't quickly stand up to flee or defend itself.

Chapter 4
Surviving in the Wild

A mother giraffe usually returns to the same place every time she gives birth to a baby.

Young Giraffes

After carrying the baby inside her body for about 14 months, a mother giraffe gives birth standing up, usually to a single calf.

A giraffe is huge from the moment it is born. A newborn calf is 6 feet tall and 150 pounds—the size of a grown man! Then it grows up to 3 inches a month until it is full size—17 feet tall and weighing 2,000 pounds. That's a ton!

Young calves are playful and love to run around together. For the first four to five months of their lives, the calves stay together in a small nursery group called a crèche. They play or rest while their mothers search for food. At least one adult female stays with the calves for protection. Young giraffes are most often attacked by predators during their first year of life. Once they are a year old, though, they have a very good chance of living to 20 to 25 years of age.

Giraffe Herds

Giraffes live in loose, open groups, often called herds, that may spread across half a mile of the savanna.

A giraffe herd may consist of mothers and their young, or be all males, or be a mix of males and females. The members of giraffe herds are constantly changing. The herds tend not to have a leader.

Most herds have up to 20 giraffes, but because of the giraffes' large size, it is not necessary for adult giraffes to live close together for mutual safety. With their extreme height and excellent eyesight, they are able to warn the others in the herd of any danger.

The home ranges of giraffes can vary greatly, anywhere from 2 square miles to 250 square miles, but average about 60 square miles—about as big as a medium-sized city. Males eventually leave their home range to mate, but females tend to stay close to the area where they were born for life.

Living in small groups helps giraffes protect themselves and their young.

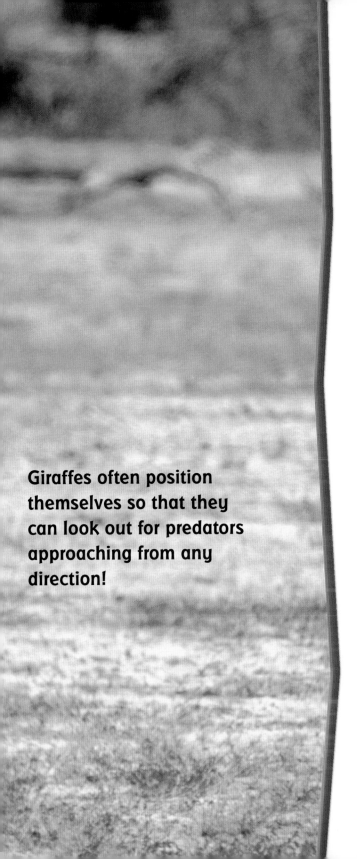

Giraffes often position themselves so that they can look out for predators approaching from any direction!

Protecting Themselves

Adult giraffes have few enemies. That's because they are so big and because the special markings on their coat help them blend in with their surroundings.

The only predators that adult giraffes fear, besides man, are lions and crocodiles. Adult giraffes are most in danger when they bend down to drink or lie down to sleep. Fortunately for giraffes, they don't need to drink very often, and they sleep for only a few minutes at a time. Giraffes also sleep standing up!

Young giraffes, though, are often preyed upon by lions, leopards, hyenas, and wild dogs. Mother giraffes protect their calves by kicking attackers with their powerful front legs, which are capable of killing a full-grown lion.

Chapter 5
Giraffes in the World

Leaf Spots

Giraffes with dark brown, leaf-shaped spots on a yellowish background are called Masai giraffes

Giraffes with large patches that are clearly outlined are called reticulated giraffes.

Spot the Spots

Although each individual giraffe has its own special color and spot pattern on its coat, scientists have identified and named roughly eight groups of giraffes that have similar patterns and share the same home range.

Some groups of giraffes have large spots, others have small ones. Certain giraffes have round spots, others have spots with sides. Spots can also be star-shaped, leaf-shaped, or no regular shape!

Only Relative

The giraffe has only one close relative, the okapi. Although the okapi has a dark coat (with no patches) and stripes on its legs, it has an elongated neck. The okapi lives in the African rain forests.

Where Giraffes Live

Although 25 million years ago giraffes lived in what is now Africa, Europe, and Asia, today's giraffes are found only in Africa, south of the Sahara Desert. Giraffes live on the savanna and in open woodlands, most often where acacia trees grow. Once hunted by humans for food, their hides, and the hair on their tails, giraffes are now protected by laws in many countries.

Fast Facts About Giraffes

Scientific name	*Giraffa camelopardalis*
Class	Mammals
Family	*Giraffidae*
Size	Males 18 feet tall
	Females 16 feet tall
Weight	Males between 2,000 and 4,000 pounds
	Females between 1,500 and 2,600 pounds
Habitat	Savannas and open woodlands with tall trees
Speed	Up to 30 miles per hour

A Giraffe Is Not a Camel!

Despite its scientific name, *Giraffa camelopardalis*, the giraffe is not related to the camel. When giraffes were first brought to Rome, they were believed to be a type of camel with spots. Today we know that giraffes are a unique species.

The word *giraffe* comes from an old Arab word meaning "one who walks swiftly."

Glossary of Wild Words

acacia   a tree that grows in warm areas and has feather-like leaves

blood vessels   the arteries and veins in a body through which blood flows to and from the heart

calf   a baby or young giraffe

cud   food that comes back into an animal's mouth from the stomach for the animal to chew again

ducts   passages or tubes in which liquid or air flows

groom   to clean fur, skin, or feathers by an animal

habitat   the natural environment where an animal or plant lives

herbivore   an animal that eats only plants

mammal   an animal with a backbone and hair on its body that drinks milk from its mother when it is born

42

mane   hair on the head or neck of an animal

predator   an animal that hunts and eats other animals to survive

prey   animals that are hunted by other animals for food

ruminants   hoofed mammals that have four chambers in their stomachs and that chew cud

savanna   a flat grassland area with scattered trees in a hot region of the world

species   a group of plants or animals that are the same in many ways

splay   to spread outward in an awkward way

swivel   to twist or turn around on the same spot

valve   a device that starts or stops the flow of liquid

Index